W9-CZJ-043

Wood to Paper

B.J. Best

Cavendish Square

New York

Published in 2017 by Cavendish Square Publishing, LLC
243 5th Avenue, Suite 136, New York, NY 10016

Copyright © 2017 by Cavendish Square Publishing, LLC

First Edition

No part of this publication may be reproduced, stored in a retrieval system, or transmitted in any form or by any means—electronic, mechanical, photocopying, recording, or otherwise—without the prior permission of the copyright owner. Request for permission should be addressed to Permissions, Cavendish Square Publishing, 243 5th Avenue, Suite 136, New York, NY 10016. Tel (877) 980-4450; fax (877) 980-4454.

Website: cavendishsq.com

This publication represents the opinions and views of the author based on his or her personal experience, knowledge, and research. The information in this book serves as a general guide only. The author and publisher have used their best efforts in preparing this book and disclaim liability rising directly or indirectly from the use and application of this book.

CPSIA Compliance Information: Batch #CW17CSQ

All websites were available and accurate when this book was sent to press.

Library of Congress Cataloging-in-Publication Data

Names: Best, B. J., 1976- author.
Title: Wood to paper / BJ Best.
Description: New York : Cavendish Square Publishing, [2017] | Series: How it is made
Identifiers: LCCN 2016030473 (print) | LCCN 2016031834 (ebook) | ISBN 9781502621146 (pbk.) | ISBN 9781502621153 (6 pack) | ISBN 9781502621160 (library bound) | ISBN 9781502621177 (Ebook)
Subjects: LCSH: Papermaking--Juvenile literature. | Pulping--Juvenile literature.
Classification: LCC TS1105.5 .B47 2017 (print) | LCC TS1105.5 (ebook) | DDC 676--dc23
LC record available at https://lccn.loc.gov/2016030473

Editorial Director: David McNamara
Copy Editor: Rebecca Rohan
Associate Art Director: Amy Greenan
Designer: Alan Sliwinski
Production Assistant: Karol Szymczuk
Photo Research: J8 Media

The photographs in this book are used by permission and through the courtesy of: Cover (Left) Mors/Shutterstock.com, (Right) LI CHAOSHU/Shutterstock.com; p. 5 Robin Bush/Getty Images; p. 7 Justin Kase/z12z/Alamy Stock Photo; p. 9 Henk Rostohar/CC-BY-SA-2.5; Released under the GNU Free Documentation License/File:Fibersorter.JPG/Wikimedia Commons; p. 11 JEAN-CHRISTOPHE VERHAEGEN/AFP/Getty Images; p. 13 Dan Lee/Alamy Stock Photo; p. 15 JG Photography/Alamy Stock Photo; p. 17, 21 Bloomberg/Getty Images; p. 19 morenosoppelsa/iStock/Thinkstock.

Printed in the United States of America

Contents

How Paper Is Made **4**

New Words **22**

Index **23**

About the Author **24**

JUL 1 8 2017

Paper can be made from wood.

The wood is cut into small pieces.

5

New paper can be made
from old paper.

Old paper is **recycled**.

It is shredded.

7

The wood or old paper is cooked with steam.

It becomes **fiber**.

Water is added to make **pulp**.

Pulp is a slush of water and fiber.

11

The pulp is washed
and cleaned.

13

The pulp is sprayed onto a moving screen.

Water dries from the pulp.

The pulp becomes a mat of paper.

15

The paper moves through hot **rollers**.

The paper gets dry.

17

The paper is made into
big rolls.

19

The paper is cut.

It is ready to use!

21

New Words

fiber (FY-ber) A thin and strong piece. It is like a thread.

pulp (PULP) A mix of water and wood or old paper.

recycled (ree-SY-kulled) Used again.

roller (ROLL-er) A large, round bar.

Index

cooked, 8

fiber, 8, 10

pulp, 10, 12, 14

recycled, 6
roller, 16

shredded, 6

water, 10, 14

About the Author

B.J. Best lives in Wisconsin with his wife and son. He has written several other books for children. He has made paper at home.

About BOOKWORMS

Bookworms help independent readers gain reading confidence through high-frequency words, simple sentences, and strong picture/text support. Each book explores a concept that helps children relate what they read to the world they live in.